Humor

75 YEARS OF
THE COMICS

Richard Felton Outcault, "Buster Brown," 1908. This original drawing was presented to Colonel William "Buffalo Bill" Cody in 1908. Courtesy of the Buffalo Bill Memorial Museum, Golden, Colorado.

75 YEARS OF THE COMICS

INTRODUCTION BY MAURICE HORN

BOSTON BOOK & ART/*Publisher*

Boston, Mass.

THE NEW YORK CULTURAL CENTER

in association with Fairleigh Dickinson University

New York, N.Y.

Contents

ACKNOWLEDGMENTS

Many people have helped in the preparation of this exhibition. We especially wish to thank the following persons who have generously contributed time and effort as well as the use of their collections: Richard Marshall, John Herbert, Woody Gelman, Tony Sanguino, Michel Greg, Bill Blackbeard, Art Spiegelman, Milton Caniff, Will Eisner, Burne Hogarth, Art Wood, Leonard Darvin, Jay Lynch, Carl Burgos, Alain Saint-Ogan, Jessie Kahles Straut.

We would also like to thank the following organizations for their cooperation: King Features Syndicate, United Feature Syndicate, Publishers-Hall Syndicate, Chicago Tribune-New York News Syndicate, The Comics Magazine Association of America, Marvel Comics Group, National Periodical Publications, Archie Comics, Editions du Lombard, Editions Dupuis, Editions Dargaud, Editions Azur, Beaverbrook Newspapers, EDIP-Milano, Buru Lan S.A. de Ediciones, Charlton Comics, and the Academy of Comic Book Arts.

We extend our particular thanks to Maurice Horn, whose wide knowledge and efforts contributed greatly to organizing "75 Years of the Comics," and to the trustees of the New York Cultural Center, whose cooperation helped to make it a reality.

Donald Karshan,
Director
The New York Cultural Center

Introduction: What is Comic Art?

It is the fate of most new art forms to be greeted with derision. The laughter has been longest and loudest against the comics. No other form (except the movies) holds such fascination and appeal for the general public, none is so American in its expression, yet none has suffered so much neglect, scorn, and ignorance from the American art establishment.

The comics reach almost daily into nearly every home in the Western World, and well beyond. They constitute a genuine sociological and cultural phenomenon that has already spanned over three-quarters of a century. Yet, as a new form of expression—at once bewildering in its variety of genres and styles and reassuring in its simplicity of design and purpose—the comics deserve a serious critical consideration.

The Beginnings: Europe

Many well-meaning but artistically naïve apologists of the form, and quite a few artistically knowledgeable detractors as well, have claimed for the comics an ancient and noble lineage, from the cave paintings of Altamira and Lascaux through the Egyptian bas-reliefs, the Babylonian steles, and the Pompeian murals to the Books of the Saints and the *Biblia Pauperum* of the Middle Ages. It is true that some of these efforts (often accidentally) introduced narrative innovations that were to be put to good use by later artists. However, these did not point to a new direction in artistic communication but merely refined old and often archaic forms. Ontological postulation is as meaningless in this domain as in others and cannot substitute for an analytical inquiry into the forces and motivations that helped shape the new medium.

Only after the Renaissance, which rekindled old dreams and stirred up new ones, did there develop a methodical search for a new medium that would intimately fuse—not simply juxtapose—narrative and picture into one comprehensive form. After a few inconclusive experiments along these lines, the eighteenth century saw the creation and rapid popularization of the "cartoon" (from the French *carton*, a sketch or study on pasteboard), which was a drawing of political, satirical, or merely humorous purpose, containing within one frame a self-explanatory scene accompanied by a caption or a brief text. In thus blending text and picture to form a single visual experience, the cartoon is the first legitimate ancestor of the comics, and the very word "cartoon" has become an integral part of its vocabulary.

This method found its fullest expression in England, where Thomas Rowlandson and William Hogarth created sequences of these cartoons centered round a unifying theme (Hogarth's "The Rake's Progress" is probably the best known of the cartoon series). More significantly, these artists made a systematic use of the "balloon," a cloud-shape issuing from the lips of the characters, enclosing dialogue. Later James Gillray was to refine these techniques and spread them to the Continent.

Subsequently Europe saw a veritable flood of illustrated narratives whose effect was to be felt all through the nineteenth century. Diversely called, "images populaires," or "histoires en images," or "Bilderbogen," they did not, however, make full use of the innovations of the English artists. None of them employed the balloon for instance, but put a text, sometimes of very substantial size, underneath each separate picture, thereby again divorcing the narrative from its pictorial support. This was the case of even the Swiss Rodolphe Töppfer, whose *Histoires en Estampes* otherwise reveal an uncanny ability to weave a brilliantly graphic narrative round the redundant text.

The German Wilhelm Busch and the French Christophe (George Colomb) also contributed to the nascent art of the comics, the former in his creation of the two unforgettable characters *Max und Moritz*, the latter in his sure delineation of action and his use of movement to link his different pictures together.

However promising, these experiments were to come to a dead end. In their almost slavish devotion to the written word, the European artists did not or would not comprehend the liberating power of the image. Their problems were further compounded by the incomprehension of the public, who looked upon their work as something not quite respectable. Thus the picture-story seemed to have joined the ranks of unsuccessful artistic experiments with which the nineteenth century is replete.

The Birth of the Form: America

Unlike Europe, the United States did not cultivate to any such extent the tradition of genteel literariness. American newspapers and magazines displayed a robust and sometimes rambunctious vitality to which editorial cartoonists and pictorial reporters contributed their legitimate share. The Civil War was brought in vivid detail to the American public through the illustrated pages of *Frank Leslie's Illustrated* and *Harper's Bazaar*, just as Frederic Remington and Charles Schreyvogel would later pictorially chronicle the opening of the western frontier.

Particularly significant was the popularity of the humor magazines: *Puck, Judge, Life*, in whose pages it was already possible to discover the artists who would later become famous through the comics: Richard Outcault, James Swinnerton, F. B. Opper. At the same time, the American daily newspapers, competing for readership, brought forth the Sunday supplements, which made increasingly generous use of illustration and color. Now, almost at the end of the century, all conditions seemed to be right for the bursting forth of a new form of communication, neither literature nor merely graphic art, but borrowing freely from both.

To answer the growing demand for illustrators and cartoonists (the term had already come into general use), new and sometimes untried talent was brought to the fore, producing the necessary artistic ferment required for all radical departures from the accepted norm. The importing of new and more advanced presses from Europe allowed the newspapers to print more copies better and faster, and to reach for an ever-increasing public. The enormous influx of immigrants from eastern and southern Europe, with little or no knowledge of the English language, gave the medium of visual communication a steady and safe public, free from the shibboleths of literary forms. Finally, the circulation wars among newspapers also worked to the advantage of the artist, who, unlike his writing colleague, had a style that was recognizable at first glance.

The often-recounted struggle of Joseph Pulitzer and William Randolph Hearst for hegemony over the New York market, with the protagonists luring employees away from each other and putting more and more reliance on their Sunday supplements, provided the final catalyst in the synthesis of the disparate elements of narrative and illustration. In a matter of months a new form was born. As I have elsewhere* stated: "The comic strip, child of commercialism and technology, inadvertently conceived and born by accident, was to grow and proliferate in all directions before anyone even thought of giving it a name."

Even the exact date of this birth has caused much quibbling among specialists, although the consensus of opinion places it in the year 1896, with the appearance of Outcault's *Yellow Kid* in its definitive version. It is appropriate therefore to celebrate today the seventy-fifth birthday of the comics.

The Founding Fathers

As happens with most artistic pioneers, the early American cartoonists labored in a critical obscurity that sharply contrasted with their popular fame. It was just as well that the taste-makers of the day left the comics alone: their first practitioners were rough and coarse, often vulgar, but full of vitality and élan, with the heady ideas and bold concepts of the genuine primitive. Egged on by their publishers and trying to outdo one another in daring and innovation, these instinctive masters almost unwittingly shaped a new form. But is it art? Only the middlebrow critic will stick to the distinction between "high" and "low" art. It is undeniable that the artists of the comics displayed a

A History of the Comic Strip.

mastery, however uncouth, and a self-expression, however unformed, that one would rarely find in most of the "art" of the turn of the century.

Both Outcault and Swinnerton can lay claim to the distinction of having been the "inventor" of the comics. As early as 1892 Swinnerton had created *Little Bears and Tigers,* a series depicting in a continuing sequence of weekly appearances the adventures of a merry crew of assorted animal characters, thus renewing and updating the great cartoon tradition of the English masters. Outcault used text and dialogue enclosed within the picture and, of course, the success of his *Yellow Kid* (from which the term "yellow journalism" is derived) definitely established the viability of the form.

The greatest contributor to the new medium however, was Rudolph Dirks whose *Katzenjammer Kids* (loosely based on Busch's *Max und Moritz*) was the first comic to integrate Swinnerton's and Outcault's discoveries (or rediscoveries) and to make full and systematic use of the balloon as main support for the accompanying dialogue. Indeed, thanks to Dirk's efforts, the balloon became the instantly recognizable trademark of the comic strip. It is noteworthy that this remarkable series is still in existence after almost three-quarters of a century, but is now done by very unremarkable artists.

It fell to F. B. Opper (who, unlike the twenty-year-old Dirks, was already a cartoonist of some distinction) to sum up the possibilities of the form. Coming at a later date (1899) he thus had the benefit of hindsight and could more easily transform the comic strip into the perfect vehicle of his vision and ideas. His best remembered creation, *Happy Hooligan,* perhaps represents the epitome of the early comics strip and was to a considerable extent responsible for the direction the comics were to take.

Thus the four artists mentioned above can rightly be called the fathers of the comics (with W. R. Hearst as the unlikely godfather). Around 1900, thanks to the pioneering spirit of these men, the comics were already in possession of a basic vocabulary and a recognizable set of conventions, and were evolving their own vital syntax. The whole process took place in a matter of a few years, truly a remarkable achievement.

The Comics: A Working Definition

What is comic art? It is already possible to give a tentative answer to this question. Coulton Waugh in his pioneering book *The Comics* (1947) first propounded an analytical definition which came to be widely accepted as the groundwork on which to build any serious study of the comics. Summarily put, the comics are a form necessarily including the following elements: a narrative told by a sequence of pictures, a continuing cast of characters, and the inclusion of dialogue or text within the picture.

Unfortunately, Waugh and his subsequent followers did not fully comprehend the significance of their discovery. Instead of realizing that they had just described the broad features of a new art form calling for a new set of standards, they kept trying to fit this newcomer into the alien mold of older and accepted forms. It is therefore not surprising that this conceptual aberration led its authors further and further into aesthetic confusion. Thus Waugh at the conclusion of his extensive study asked: "Is artistic and literary development [in the comics] possible?" to which he answered "yes," hardly an earth-shaking pronouncement at the end of a volume of 360 pages.

Aside from the naïveté of believing that content could somehow develop independently from form and structure (and elaborate structure at that), Waugh and his followers correlatively failed to recognize that the descriptive definition they themselves had given precluded any centrifugal development and that all subsequent improvements had to be organic to this pre-existent and self-contained form. Within the external structure of the comics there had to be an internal cohesiveness, knowledge of which could not be gained from surface observation.

The above definition, then, does not give us insight into the essence of the comics any more than the formula for π gives us knowledge of the nature of the circle. As a methodological tool, it can be of invaluable usefulness. By clearing away much of the semantic confusion surrounding the comics, it narrows the scope of research and puts the subject into a more accurate, more sharply defined, focus.

The Language of the Comics

It would not occur to the serious critic to judge a novel on the evidence of a few paragraphs, or a play on the basis of one or two scenes. Yet this summary practice is widely accepted in the criticism of the comics. Somehow, few art critics have accepted the simple and legitimate notion that a comic feature should be judged within its proper context and on its own terms. In other words, a working knowledge of the *language* of the comics is necessary for any intelligent discussion of the subject, and, because this is specialized knowledge, many a critic who set out to expose the new form succeeded only in exposing his own ignorance.

Even when honestly trying to judge the comics, the unwitting critic is likely to evaluate the text and the artwork independently whereas the most original feature of the form is that it blends these two elements into one organic whole. Expression in the comics is the result of this interaction between word and picture, it is the product and not the sum of its component parts. The drawing and the text reinforce (or pull down) each other in a variety of ways. When the writing (plot, situations, dialogue) is good, it can carry passable or even poor art; conversely, good art can sometimes make up for any weakness in the writing. When both art and writing are exceptional, the result is a masterpiece (George Herriman's *Krazy Kat* is one good example). When art and writing both are terrible, the result validates all the criticisms leveled at the comics. Unfortunately, as in all art forms, the bad is much more common than the good.

The basic element in the language of the comics is the panel, a simple drawing (with or without accompanying text or dialogue) most often enclosed in a rectangular or square frame, that stands both in isolation from and in intimate relation to the others, like a word in a sentence. This is the simplest form (in the strict sense of *Gestalt*) of the comics, the contents of which are perceived as one unit. It is therefore futile to try to judge the artistry of a comic by the drawing in one panel (or a number of panels, each examined in isolation). To separate image content from narrative content is to do violence to the whole concept of the art.

The panels themselves are grouped, again like words in a sentence, into strips (superficially, a horizontal succession of panels) or pages, whose format widely varies but whose chief characteristic, as opposed to the strip, is to present a vertical as well as a horizontal combination of frames. In turn, these strips and pages are articulated in a more or less complex manner into sequences and episodes.

For their vocabulary, the comics borrow freely both from common language and the language of representational art. Over the years, moreover, they have developed a peculiar set of conventions, of which the balloon is the most widely known and used, and invented an array of new signs and symbols, mainly in the form of word-pictures and visual puns. Thus a lamp comes to represent a bright idea, a black cloud over the head of a character, a feeling of grief or despair. Such examples are endless.

Today the language of the comics with its innovations, its symbols, its colorful onomatopoeia (pow, vroom, ka-boom!) is as familiar and commonly accepted as the language of the movies. Together they have forced upon western man a new way of looking at external reality.

The Comics as Communication

Even before the advent of Marshall McLuhan, the comics were usually viewed as a means of communication, without much attention to them as art, whether actual or potential. There is some validity in seeing the comics exclusively in this light, and this prejudice has been reinforced in no small measure by those organizations engaged in selling the comics as a product. (The same attitude was also prevalent among the movie studios toward motion pictures, and it contributed largely to the demise of Hollywood.)

The two main supports of the comics have historically been the book and the newspaper, and this has resulted in the development of two different publics, with some overlapping between them. As the heir of the picture book, the book of comics (and later the comic book, narrowly defined) addressed itself mainly to younger readers, while the comic strip, being part and parcel of the daily newspaper, had generally been conceived as a more adult form of expression. However, the gap has been narrowing over the years with the appearance, in the United States of comic books destined mainly for adults, and in Europe, of illustrated weeklies encompassing a greater range of features. One of these papers styles itself, fittingly enough, "The newspaper of young people from 7 to 77."

There is no doubt that the public reads the comics primarily for their entertainment value; but even so we must make a distinction between a routine readership (the reader who turns to the comics page from force of habit upon opening his newspaper) and an active readership, which consists in looking in the comics for some form of specific satisfaction (it might be artistic, or nostalgic, or even campy). We find that those adults most interested in the comics are located at either end of the educational spectrum. It would seem that the less educated enjoy the comics for their uncomplicated immediacy, while the sophisticates have increasingly adopted the medium (first in Europe and now in the United States) for its anticultural qualities. If the medium is the message, then the message of the comics, with their flouting of the rules of traditional art and of civilized language, can only be subversion.*

A word must be said about the comics as specialized communication. They have been used in advertising ever since the *Yellow Kid*, and their utilization as propaganda has also been widespread, from the crude flag-waving of French comics in World War I to Steve Canyon and Buz Sawyer fighting the good fight in Vietnam and American "imperialist" soldiers being lambasted in Red Chinese comics (yes, there is such a thing). Among its more sedate functions, the medium has been used in the dissemination of information (*Dennis the Menace and Dirt* for the Soil Conservation Society of America and *Cliff Merritt Sets The Record Straight* for the Brotherhood of Railroad Trainmen for instance), and as a valuable teaching tool. Two recent textbooks prepared by the University of Illinois for teaching the new math rely heavily on the comic form.

Compared to other mass media, the comics are not a highly effective instrument for either suasion or enlightenment. They are not as impressive as the movies, nor as authoritative as the written word, nor as pervasive as television. That they function best as a form of artistic expression may be a commercial drawback, but this very fact also testifies to the integrity of the form.

The Semantic Confusion about the Comics

As has happened with the cinema, the popular

*This point in one form or the other has always been the leading argument of the enemies of the comics. Now it is being utilized *a contrario* by the exponents of the counterculture.

success of the comics as a mass medium has obscured their pre-existence as a form. Surveying the forest but ignoring the individual trees, the critics have seized upon the comics as a sociological subject for clinical study, thus denying *a priori* that aesthetic qualities could be attributed to them. This of course has helped conceal the social critic's ignorance of the dynamics of creation in the comics.

Actually, the comics are a much more personal mode of expression than the movies, television, or even most modern manifestations of art and music. Whether there are several authors or only one, each feature is done in a craftsmanlike manner, not only (as would be expected), the writing and the drawing, but also the lettering and the tracing of the balloons, and quite often the delineating of the frames surrounding each panel. While there exist some chemically pretreated materials, the cartoonist's instruments still remain primarily ink, pen, brush, and paper. This of course does not give a comic a personal look, unless the artist has a personal message to convey, but it serves to prove that the comics are far from being the mechanized process that some pretend it to be. It is true that the comics are often a team effort, with assistants working on the backgrounds, the lettering, even the inking, and there is no denying that more often than not it is a case of too many cooks spoiling the broth. Predictably enough, the best authors are those who retain the strongest direction (Charles Schulz, for instance, does everything on *Peanuts*, including the lettering), and therefore they give their features the most achieved sense of unity.

Because artistic creation is present (or at least potential) in every aspect of the comics, the temptation is great to apply to this new form the canons of traditional aesthetics, but here again there is the danger of intellectual confusion. Because the comics present so many facets, each mirroring the rules of different art forms, they present some thorny epistemological problems that must first be cleared away before we can get at any understanding of the form.

The Comics as Graphic Art

Since a comic, any comic, is first perceived visually, custom has always classified the comics as graphic art and linked them (dumped them, would be more accurate) with illustration and caricature. And indeed, as we have seen, there is a direct kinship between the cartoon and the comic strip, just as there is a strong bond between the story strip and illustration. The differences, however, are just as obvious: the cartoon and the illustration concentrate on only one point, whether a punch line or the dramatic highlight in a narrative, while the comics must keep up the continuity of a whole sequence.

This is not meant to play down the artistic skills required to draw a comic feature. Karl Fortess' assertions* that "the comic strip artist is not concerned with art problems, problems of form, spatial relationships, and the expressive movement of line" and that "the comic strip has failed to produce a Daumier or a Hogarth" are nonsense. The best of the comic artists are very much concerned with artistic problems, although from a different vantage point than that of the traditional draftsman. On this score I will simply let the illustrations in this catalogue speak for themselves. As for excellence of drawing, the comics can boast of a long line of outstanding artists from Winsor McCay to Hogarth (Burne Hogarth) to Guido Crepax. All artistic currents have found expression in the comics, and a collection of the best works in this field present an astonishing retrospective of the history of graphic art.

It would thus be perfectly feasible to judge the comics entirely on their artistic merits, just as it would be to judge a motion picture on its photography alone. It would mean, of course, that we are willing to place undue restrictions on other ways of appreciating the comics. As we have seen, the image in the comics is not fixed in some point in time but inserts itself within the time-flow of the narrative. It is a *diffuse* image whose projection in space, overlapping from one frame to another, mirrors a projection in time, forward and backward. Owing to that fact, the artistic concerns of the comic artist are not wholly coincidental with the concerns of the traditional artist, and it is only axiomatic to conclude that traditional aesthetics cannot be wholly coincidental with the aesthetics of the comics.

The Comics as Narrative Literature

Functionally, the comics would seem to belong

*"The Comics as Non-Art", in *The Funnies: An American Idiom.*

to some literary discipline, as they are chiefly meant to be *read*, and the persistent public indifference to silent or pantomime strips bears this out. Some critics, therefore, have tried to link the comics with folk literature. There again similarities may be found; certainly, the argument of many a comic sequence closely parallels such folk forms as the tale, the fable, or the parable. Harold Gray in *Little Orphan Annie*, Al Capp in *Li'l Abner*, and Walt Kelly in *Pogo* show a special fondness for these forms. As we have seen, however, the comics are the expression of individual artists and so run counter to the collective processes that have contributed to the vast body of folk literature. What the comic artists have done is simply to weave inchoate or unformed mythologies into their own scheme of things, in ways not dissimilar to those of artists and writers everywhere.

Narration, however defined, remains the essence of the comics: their purpose is to tell a story. Because they aim at a large public, the comics have come to compete with and eventually displace older forms of popular literature, such as the dime novels, the pulps, the magazine serials. Their superiority over these earlier forms comes not, as is widely assumed, from the fact that they can tell the story in graphic terms, but from the fact that, because of their graphic elucidation of detail and background, they can tell the story in more economical terms. As some wit has put it, "They give you more bangs in less time."

Building on these premises, some authors have tried to fashion their comics into monumental novels, with all that implies in terms of a self-contained universe governed by its own laws, dynamics, and motivations. It would do them injustice to compare them exclusively with the picaresque novels. Some have deliberately aimed higher. Harold Gray's *Little Orphan Annie* offers perhaps the closest example of a novel in comic form. Not only are there undertones of Dickens and Hugo, but the obsessing and rhythmic repetition of motif and echo is very close to the preoccupations of modern novelists. In *Gasoline Alley* Frank King set out to describe the life and times of a small midwestern community with a tenderness and serenity worthy of Goethe's *Wilhelm Meister*. Other examples could be cited with equal justification.

If I have insisted on the literary qualities present in the comics, it is because they are not so readily apparent as are their graphic values. There again we should be careful not to beg the question and judge the comics in terms of literary standards alone. The comics are indeed a literary form, but one that should not be reduced to its literary elements, lest we subvert its very *raison d'être*.

The Comics as Dramatic Form

A case may also be made (and indeed has been made) for the comics being a latter-day outgrowth of the dramatic arts. It may be said without irony that the comics, more than any other twentieth-century literary form, follow Aristotle's rule of a beginning, a middle, and an end. They have indeed kept close to the rules of dramatic construction and have accordingly, in the seventy-five years of their existence, accomplished much the same progression as western drama since the Middle Ages. Starting with the farce or pantomime (*Yellow Kid, Katzenjammer Kids, Happy Hooligan*) they have assimilated the elements of the comedy of observation and manners (*Bringing Up Father, Moon Mullins*) before proceeding to the themes of the social comedy and the melodrama (*Mary Worth, Steve Canyon*) and the drama of ideas (*Little Orphan Annie*). The great dramatic currents of the twentieth century have also found their representatives in the comics with George Herriman, Walt Kelly, Jules Feiffer.

The argument should not be slighted. Owing to the ubiquitous balloon, the dialogue constitutes the strongest and most prominent literary feature of the comics. While most cartoonists use dialogue chiefly as a means to convey essential information and to carry the plot forward, many others are aware of its dramatic force and have played skillfully on it. They have called upon dialogue to establish character and motivation (George McManus, Milton Caniff, Hergé), to create suspense and anticipation (Harold Gray, Allen Saunders, Caniff again), to reveal the central themes and ideas of their work (George Herriman, Walt Kelly, Charles Schulz), to establish tone and rhythm, and to give purpose to the action. The examples are endless, but dramatic conventions and stage devices are the special domain of two artists, George McManus and Walt Kelly, whose work has always been more dramatic than narrative.

In the context of the action, the balloon plays an ambivalent role: by function, it is a dramatic device, by nature, a graphic form, thus it creates possibilities that great cartoonists have been prompt to explore. By using the graphic elements of the balloon (its shape, the lettering, and the symbols within it) in a literal way, they are able to translate the nonverbal aspects of language: tone, intensity, rhythm, accent. More importantly, the balloon can transcend speech, addressing itself to the naked thought (the thought balloon), and even free itself of all the restraints of organized expression. Thus we see the balloon changing its form, slowly dissolving, or suddenly exploding. We see it used as a ploy, a mask, a shield, as an attack weapon. Here again we see an analogy with the symbolic use of props in the modern theater.

Comics and Cinema

For many reasons, some already mentioned, the comics come closer to the movies than to any other art form. Not only were they both born around the same time and from the same artistic and commercial preoccupations, but also they both tend to the same end: the creation of dialectical movement, either through optical illusion (cinema) or through kinetic suggestion (comics). It is well to point out at this juncture that many techniques which have come to be called "cinematic" have originated in the comics. Montage was the rule in the comics well before Eisenstein came along, and the techniques of cutting, framing, and panning were already used by such early practitioners as Opper, McCay, and Feininger. As for the "audio" aspect, the comics had ample time to develop the voice-off, the voice-over, and the overlapping dialogue during the thirty years when the movies had at their disposal only the barbarous subtitle. Even the grammars of the comics and the movies are almost identical: the concepts of "shot" (as opposed to the static "scene") and of "sequence," and the attending variations of angles and perspectives, the unlimited possibilities of tracking forward and backward, are present in both forms.

The influence of the movies on the comics has been very great. Not only have they given the comics better techniques for the suggestion of movement in transposing on paper the equivalent of cinema lighting, depth of field, silhouetted background, etc., but they have also proved to be a main source of inspiration. The movie serials were as much the forerunners of the adventure strip as the dime novel or the pulps, and their distinctive syncopated rhythm was to become the hallmark of most of the action series of the thirties.

This constant cross-fertilization was soon to produce its first legitimate offshoot: the animated cartoon, a peculiarly modern marriage of art and technology. In their book *The Cinema as Art*, Ralph Stephenson and J. R. Debrix declare that "the accepted definition of an animated film is, not that it is drawn by hand, but that it is created frame-by-frame." This is how the comics are created also. It accounts for the fact that the animated cartoon owes more to the comics than to the cinema, but a discussion of this subject would go beyond the scope of this introduction to the art.

A Search for New Standards

By now it must have become increasingly apparent that the comics cannot be reduced to fit into any preconceived formula. By their very existence they seem to baffle any attempt at epistemological elucidation and to offer an obdurate resistance to traditional aesthetics. One can very well sympathize with the resentment and frustration of the critic who finds all his neat little formulas of little or no use in any true explication of the medium. The comics simply refuse to be pigeonholed. One solution (and it is the most frequent, if the least enlightening) is to put the comics beyond the pale, to write them off as non-art, non-literature, and non-significant. This approach was tried on the movies also, and to the astonishment of only the ignorant, both comics and movies have been able to survive the excommunication of the would-be defenders of Art, Truth, Beauty, and the preservation of the cultural status quo.

A peculiar form of intellectual perversity consists of doggedly trying to berate the comics in the name of art or literature, in the face of overwhelming evidence that the comics do not conform to either. We are in presence of an altogether new and original form, whose intrinsic values must be objectively assessed. This is no easy task, hardly easier that it has been with the movies. A thorough knowledge of the field must be obtained, with the same assiduity as is required of any other discipline; the a priori judgment that this is an inferior form only deserving of inferior scholarship is an especially galling piece of tortuous reasoning. Only by serious study can we arrive at an understanding of the underlying structures of the comics, without which no critical conclusion can emerge.

Space and Time in the Comics

The problems of spatial representation have been bedeviling the comic artist ever since the inception of the medium. Because the cartoonist deals not with one picture but with an organic sequence of pictures, these problems cannot be solved by perspective alone, since simple perspective would give the same depth value to all the panels, thus it would flatten them out, giving them the same appearance as the friezes on the walls of Egyptian mastabas. Some artists, notably Chester Gould, have put this principle to good aesthetic use, but, in the hands of less gifted craftsmen, this only produces a succession of still drawings.

In order to create depth, other artists have resorted to the effects of chiaroscuro or to a manipulation of scale that subtly distorts traditional perspective and forces a perception of volume from the reader, much as a composed photograph does. In the Sunday pages (as well as in the comic books) foremost artists, such as Winsor McCay or Burne Hogarth, have created spatiality out of the multilinearity (horizontal, vertical, diagonal) of the layout by means of expanding or projecting the figures along carefully worked-out vectors. The drawings seem literally ready to burst out of their frames.

In the comics, time is a function of space:* the frames of a strip or page are divisions of time. Thus narrative flow (how the author conceived of the passing of time in a particular sequence), and time flow (how it is perceived by the reader), are seldom coincidental. Furthermore, they both must be weighed against actual reading time, which may

*This is their most important difference from the movies, in which space is a function of time.

be very long (as in the case of many newspaper strips) or quite short (as with a comic book). The resulting confusion further adds to the sense of unreality that comics produce. Even a feature like *Gasoline Alley*, which purports to keep pace with real time and whose characters age along with the reader, does not escape the rule.

Time in the comics seems to have no organic function; all that happens, happens not by necessity but by accident or chance. Time is limitless and open-ended, it may also be reversible: often the characters will go back ten, twenty, or more years in time and start the cycle again in a different direction. The comics are unhistorical, not because they refuse to deal with their times (they often do), but because real time is irrelevant to their purpose. There is an almost complete absence of teleology in the comics: the events that took place last year have not the slightest influence on the events taking place now, at least not in the strictly causative sense. The same may be argued of popular literature, but words have not the same suggestive power as pictures. By confronting us with a direct representation of reality, the image involves us much more closely in the process. As the Bogart cult demonstrates, only the movies might have been more effective than the comics in this respect, if actors weren't made of mortal flesh. Thus the comics are uniquely qualified to take us into a paradoxical universe, in which time is neither consumed nor abolished: it is the universe of the eternal present tense.

Themes of the Comics

Aesthetic preoccupations and commercial considerations have always conspired to limit the thematic range of the comics. Commercially, the comics are a mass medium, and their authors must give the public something immediately and easily recognizable. Yet at the same time the action must have a certain exemplarity, if it is to rise above the level of the simple anecdote. The problem of creating a milieu at once ordinary and different is the lot of all mass media that aspire to become art forms. To answer the challenge, the comics may resort to the wholesale creation of a mythical ontogeny, as in the case of Superman and most

other superheroes, or of a dream kingdom (*Little Nemo* is the best example), but few are the comics that have not made some use of the device.

The protagonists of the comics, whether by design or by necessity, go back to the fount of our collective memories and aspirations. They represent some emblematic figure, some archetype linking us to primeval drives across the night of history. They are often outcasts, outsiders, by choice or by fate: bums and adventurers (and the recent rash of "superheroes with problems") is only a clever ploy to play it both ways.* The themes built round these figures are by necessity few in number, but the variations on the primary theme are the measure of any artist. In this respect, the cartoonists display an astonishing range and an unequaled evocative power. It is as if the comics had taken it upon themselves to embody all our collective longings and to try to give them some channel for fulfillment. Yet at the same time it is asked of them that they toe the social line, and this dichotomy has often led to ambivalence and frustration.

However ridiculous the family may appear in *Bringing Up Father*, for instance, the notion of family itself is never under attack. As one press release once stated: "Jiggs never struck Maggie and will never divorce her." The same ambivalence may be noted in relation to society itself. The first comics were genuinely anarchistic and nihilistic (*The Katzenjammer Kids* is the classic example), but soon their creators learned to compromise and eventually to accept the rules of social order, however ludicrous. The free spirit of the comics could not be kept down, however, and it is now to be found among the so-called underground comics.

In one of the most revealing pages of *Pogo*, Walt Kelly says of the comics that they are "like a dream . . . a tissue of paper reveries . . . it glows and glimmers its way thru unreality, fancy an' fantasy." Even to an intellectual (by any standard) artist like Kelly, the intellectual limitations of the comics are apparent. But these limitations are also their strength. By their very inability to sustain for long any lofty or more relevant theme, they retain the virtue of timelessness, refusing thus to become another dreary exercise in ephemeral literature.

*The ritualism often noted in the comic heroes' costumes is an external clue to the effect (for example, Happy Hooligan's tin can, Mandrake's coat-and-tails, Batman's cowl).

Stylistics

Since the form and structure of the comics are probably more binding on their creators than are those of any other art form, style above all sets the great artist apart. In order to shape the two heterogeneous elements of the comics into one artistic whole, each cartoonist has had to evolve his own distinctive signature (at least those who are not merely content to become hacks drifting along with the medium do). Thus two different approaches begin to emerge: in the first, the picture takes precedence over the text, and the story is told in purely narrative and graphic terms (this method was the trademark of the great draftsmen from McCay and Feininger to Foster and Hogarth); conversely, the second solution to this stylistic problem is to give primacy to the text, as happens in such features as *Little Orphan Annie*, *Li'l Abner* and *Pogo*. On the other hand, a more fluid type of narrative emerged in the thirties, in which the use of dramatic dialogue and cinematic techniques combined to preserve a skilful if delicate balance between the literary and the graphic elements of the comics. Milton Caniff is its foremost exponent.

To maintain the integrity of a sequential narrative within the framework of contiguous but separate pictures presents another set of problems. Of course, the cartoonist can construct an exact visual correlative to the written narrative, but the redundancy and wastefulness of such a method are obvious. It would seem preferable by far to have text and picture carry the action in alternation, rather than simultaneously. Will Eisner and Milton Caniff are masters of such techniques: in their features they use verbal understatement as a counterpoint to violent visual action, or, conversely, set off visual metaphors to relieve long stretches of dialogue or monologue.

The breaking down of the story into panels and sequences is also mainly a problem of style. The comic artist may prefer the careful preparation and build-up of the action, as Harold Gray and Chester Gould do, or to collide head-on with the happenings — an aggressive approach associated more with the comic book and the underground comics. To endow his images with atmosphere, the cartoonist may choose to use solid black masses, or the ambiguous delineation of backgrounds, or, on the contrary, to resort to visual objects violently etched into the foreground. The range is infinite. In this respect, color may play an important role by calling attention to important points in the narrative; it may also help to link dialectically the different frames in a sequence by carrying the same tonal value from one picture to another.

The comics also have at their disposal the syntax of the other literary and artistic forms: iteration, distortion, amplification, stylization, etc. It is up to the artist to make a discreet use of these and other devices and to avoid the sins of overdramatization and redundancy. In the comics as in all art, less is more.

Coda

The strength of the comics lies in their faculty of constantly renewing themselves when one form seems to be played out. In the seventy-five years of their history, the comics have generated successive thematic and stylistic cycles that are easy to recognize: burlesque and caricature in the beginning, family comedy in the twenties, adventure in the thirties, war in the forties, intellectual comedy in the fifties. Now that the traditional American forms in comic book and newspaper strip alike seem to have run out of steam, the standard has been adopted by the European and the underground comics. On the heels of this new departure, let us repeat the caveat that the comics are an original, not a derivative, art form worthy of analysis and discussion on its own terms and according to its own criteria. No more (but no less) should be asked of the comics' creator than is asked of any other artist, namely, the mastery of his art.

Maurice Horn

The Heroic Period

Illustrations 1–16

All through the eighteenth and nineteenth centuries, artists of many countries have labored to perfect a form that would harmoniously combine the narrative elements present in both art and literature. The following illustrations trace the process that eventually led to the creation, at the turn of the century, of this uniquely American art form: the comics, and their rapid development in the hands of their first practitioners.

1. Image d'Epinal, *(France)*, 19th Century.

2. Rodolphe Töpffer, (Switzerland), "Monsieur Crepin," 1846.

Max und Moritz

"In with 'em!" Each wretched flopper
Headlong goes into the hopper.

„Her damit!!" Und in den Trichter
Schüttelt er die Bösewichter. –

As the farmer turns his back, he
Hears the mill go "creaky! cracky!"

Rickeracke! Rickeracke!
Geht die Mühle mit Geknacke.

3. Wilhelm Busch, (Germany),
"Max und Moritz," 1871.

Max and Moritz

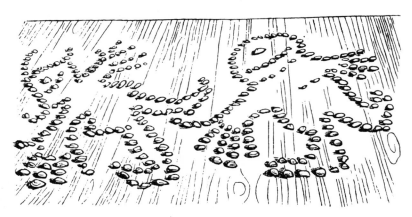

Here you see the bits *post mortem*,
Just as Fate was pleased to sort 'em.

Hier kann man sie noch erblicken
Fein geschroten und in Stücken.

Master Miller's ducks with speed

Doch sogleich verzehret sie

Gobbled up the coarse-grained feed.

Meister Müllers Federvieh.

Une imprudence d'Artémise.

Or, ces demoiselles ayant le vin gai et jugeant le moment venu de se distraire en imitant le cri de quelques animaux, un agent de la force publique leur fait remarquer fort judicieusement qu'il est l'heure de dormir et non de braire. Artémise n'hésite pas à effectuer une rotation de 180° pour exprimer en volapück, à l'agent, sa manière de voir.

L'agent, qui comprend admirablement le volapück d'Artémise, prend sa course à la poursuite de cette intelligente et gracieuse jeune fille. Il est bientôt rejoint par un second agent, puis par un troisième qui lui emboîtent le pas avec conviction et sympathie.

Puis par un quatrième, un cinquième, un sixième agent, enfin par toute la police du quartier qui, avec un zèle louable, s'empresse de suivre le mouvement. M. Fenouillard, qui croit qu'on le poursuit pour le réintégrer dans sa prison, et qui décidément, ne se sent pas de vocation pour le harakiri...

... détale avec vélocité, prestesse et distinction. Réveillés dans leur premier sommeil, les bourgeois (tant l'exemple est contagieux) suivent la foule, dans l'intention bien naturelle d'avoir des renseignements précis sur la cause de cette émotion populaire et nocturne.

Et la blonde Séléné (toujours la lune, pour les mêmes personnes que ci-devant) put, du haut du sombre azur, assister à un étrange spectacle : en effet, nos amis n'avaient pas fait 500 mètres, qu'ils avaient à leurs trousses une meute hurlante de 23 644 individus (sans compter les femmes et les petits enfants), sur lesquels 23 643 ignoraient totalement ce qu'ils faisaient là, le 23 644ᵉ l'ayant lui-même complètement oublié.

Quelques victimes du devoir.

Acculé au quai et ne se sentant décidément pas de vocation pour le harakiri, M. Fenouillard s'empresse de piquer dans l'onde amère une tête héroïque et savante.

« La femme doit suivre son mari partout où il lui plaira d'habiter. » M. Fenouillard ayant provisoirement élu domicile dans l'onde amère, madame le suit.

« Les jeunes filles bien élevées ne doivent sous aucun prétexte, quitter leurs parents », selon le précepte de la civilité puérile et honnête.

Les agents de police, au Japon, sont esclaves de leur devoir. Aussi, avec un remarquable esprit de discipline, n'hésitent-ils pas à quitter le plancher des agents pour continuer leur poursuite dans l'élément liquide.

Et les 23 644 personnes (sans compter les femmes et les petits enfants) persistent à emboîter le pas à la police, dans l'espoir d'apprendre enfin pourquoi elles courent à l'heure où les honnêtes gens dorment.

C'est pourquoi le lendemain, lorsque l'aurore aux doigts de rose ouvrit à l'ardent Phébus (c'est le Soleil ; explication nécessaire aux personnes peu fortes en mythologie, déjà nommées), ouvrit, dis-je, à l'ardent Phébus les portes d'or de l'Orient, les nautoniers repêchèrent (en comptant les femmes et les petits enfants) 44 623 cadavres 1/2, car il y avait un cul-de-jatte !

4. Christophe, (Georges Colomb), (France), "La Famille Fenouillard," 1893.

"If I gits married I got ter hustle if I wants ter keep de wolf away furninst me door."

"I'm stuck on der per-leece, an' I tink I could do it, 'cause bein' a cop is dead easy."

"Composin' music dese days is easy; all yer have ter do is ter buy Gilbert and Sullivan and de 'Chimes of Normandy' an' yez kin rite an opera."

"I might earn some money on Park Row by shakin' de bones."

"I tink I could give parlor entertainments fer de '400' or play fer de Patriarchs' ball."

"If some pretty girl wot has got a good altogether will pose fer me I'll paint a nood. I'll ask ballet girl; she's a peach."

"It costs too much to be a real sport an' win prizes at de horse show"—

—"but I tink I would be a good jockey an' a prize winner fer some one else."

"If I could jist git in ter de fish business I could make money an' live on me stock."

"Dis is one ting I wouldn't do; I would much radder work."

5. Richard F. Outcault,
"The Yellow Kid," 1896.

A STRATEGIC SCHEME THAT DIDN'T WORK.

1. "Heavens, what tobacco!"

2. "Here goes an old trick of mine."

3. "An accident, I assure you. Let me give you this perfecto."

4. "Now he'll smoke my cigar."

5. "Is he filling that pipe again?"

6. "This is too much!"

7. "You confounded villain!"

8. !!!!

6. James Swinnerton,
"Little Tiger," 1901.

MAMMA KATZENJAMMER PLAYS A BOOMERANG TRICK.
But the Kids Get Spanked Just the Same.

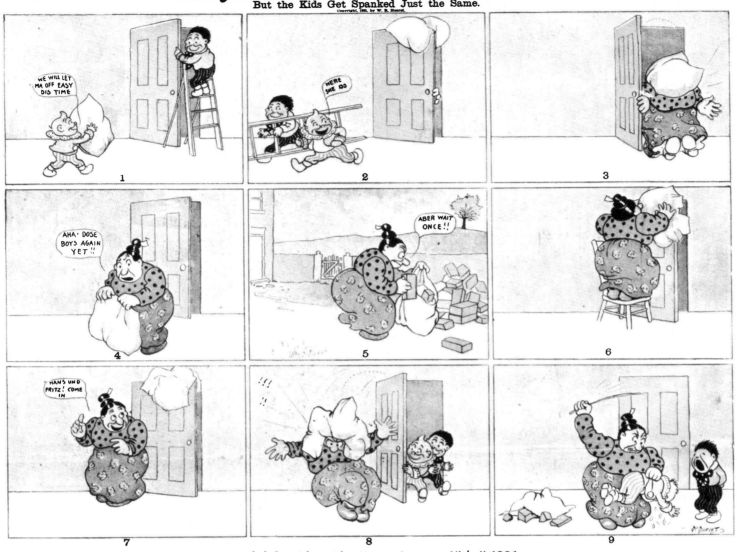

7. Rudolph Dirks, "The Katzenjammer Kids," 1901.

THE DOINGS OF HAPPY HOOLIGAN.
Talk About Heroic Life-Saving!—And Hard Luck!

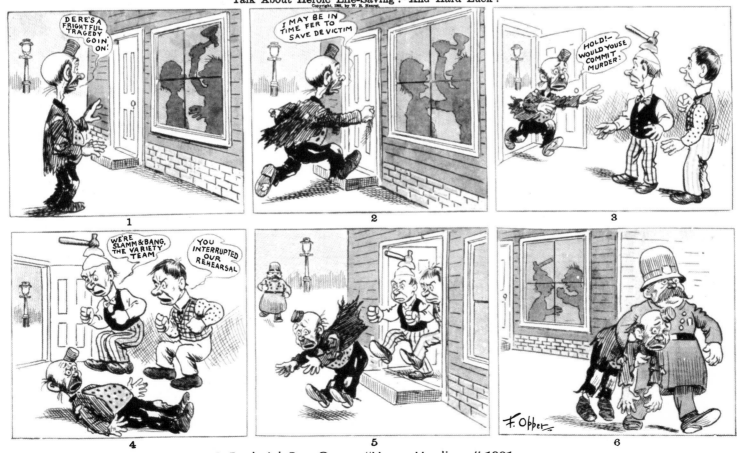

8. Frederick Burr Opper, "Happy Hooligan," 1901.

9. Gustave Verbeck,
"The Upside Downs of
Little Lady Lovekins and
Old Man Muffaroo," 1903.

10. James Swinnerton,
"Little Jimmy," 1905.

11. Silas (Winsor McCay), "The Dream of the Rarebit Fiend," 1905.

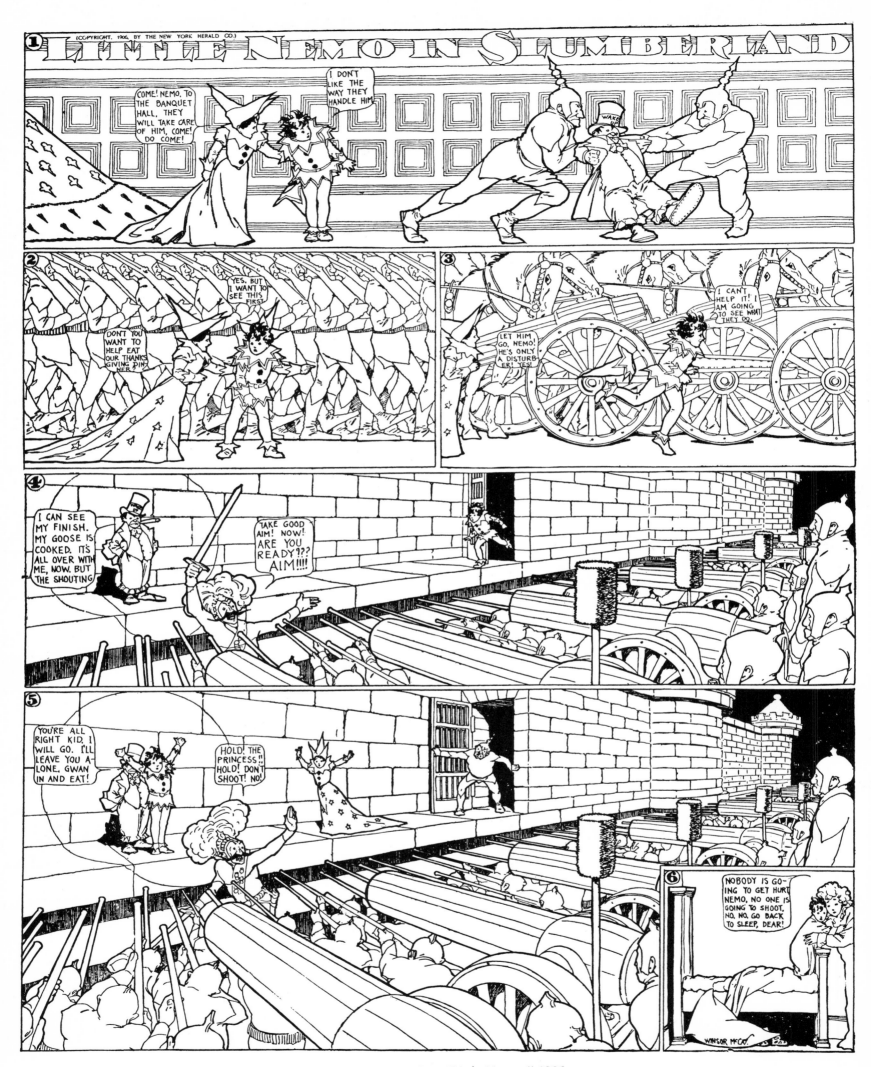

12. Winsor McCay, "Little Nemo," 1906.

13. Winsor McCay, "Little Nemo," 1907.

14. Lyonel Feininger, "Wee Willie Winkie's World," 1906.

15. Lyonel Feininger, ''The Kin-der Kids,'' 1906.

16. Richard F. Outcault, "Buster Brown," 1907.

The Great Tradition

Illustrations 17–38

Humor in its many forms has been for a long time the basic staple of the new medium; the very terms "comics" and "funnies" with which they were nicknamed derive from the observation of this simple truth. This great tradition of the comic "comics" reached its heyday in the twenties and into the thirties, when it encompassed not only the rowdy humor of the early "funnies," but a wide range of themes, from the lyrical fantasy of *Krazy Kat* to the savage satire of *Li'l Abner*.

17. George McManus, "Bringing Up Father," 1921. © King Features Syndicate.

Bringing Up Father

18. George McManus, "Bringing Up Father," 1932. © King Features Syndicate.

Boob McNutt

19. Rube Goldberg, "Boob McNutt," 1920. © King Features Syndicate.

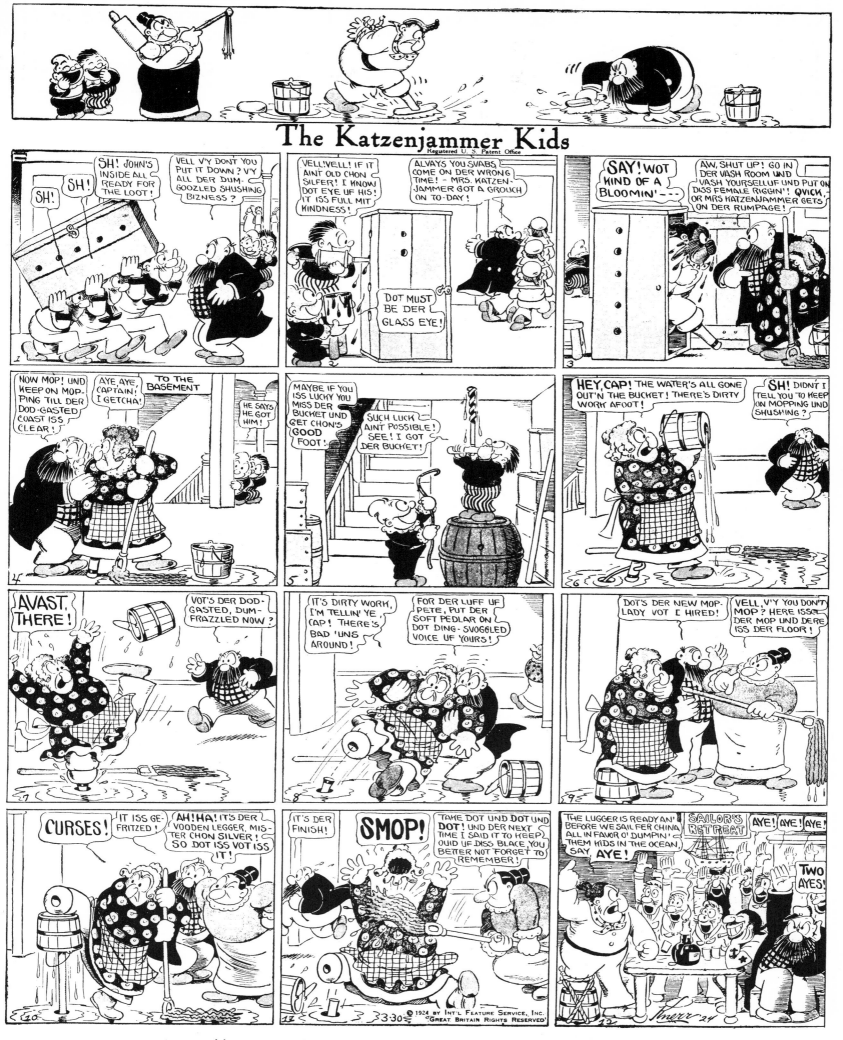

20. Harold H. Knerr, "The Katzenjammer Kids," 1924. © King Features Syndicate.

21. Willy DeBeck, "Barney Google," 1924. © King Features Syndicate.

Trade Mark, 1926, Reg. U. S. Pat. Off.

22. Milton Gross, ''Nize Baby,'' 1926. © New York World.

23. Harold Gray,
"Little Orphan Annie," 1926.
© Chicago Tribune-
New York News Syndicate.

24. Sidney Smith, "The Gumps," 1927 © Chicago Tribune-New York News Syndicate.

25. Martin Branner, "Winnie Winkle," 1927. © Chicago Tribune-New York News Syndicate.

26. Frank King, "Gasoline Alley," 1928. © Chicago Tribune-New York News Syndicate.

27. H. C. "Bud" Fisher, "Mutt and Jeff," 1930. © H. C. Fisher.

28. Frank Godwin, ''Connie,'' 1931. © Frank Godwin.

29. Chic Young, "Blondie," 1933. © King Features Syndicate.

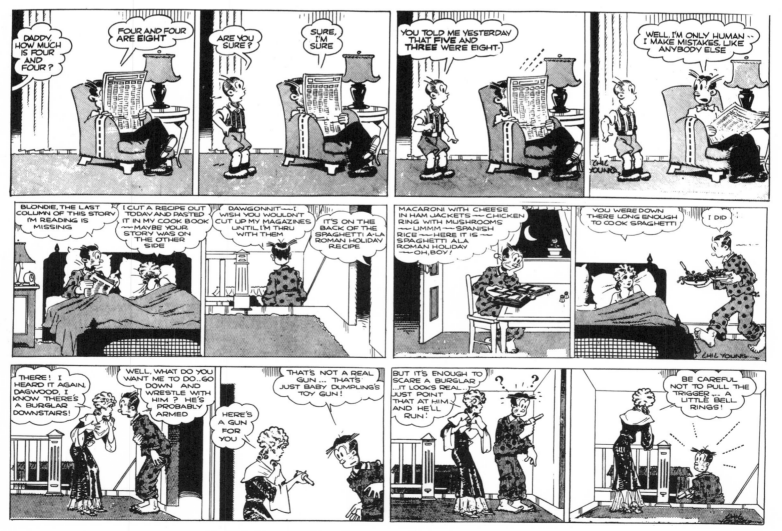

30. Chic Young, "Blondie," 1948. © King Features Syndicate.

31. Lyman Young,

"The Kid Sister," 1933.

© King Features Syndicate.

32. George Herriman, "Krazy Kat," 1937. © King Features Syndicate.

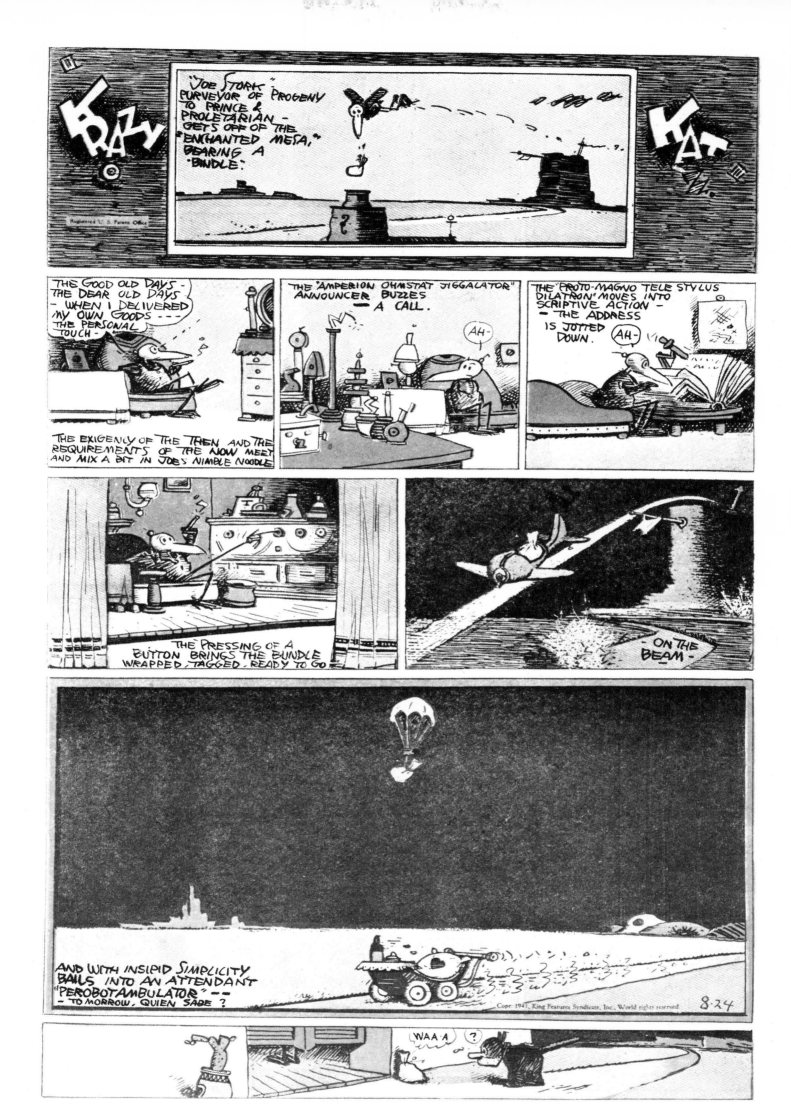

33. George Herriman, "Krazy Kat," 1941. © King Features Syndicate.

34. Elzie Segar, "Popeye," 1935. © King Features Syndicate.

35. Frank Willard,
"Moon Mullins," 1937.
© Chicago Tribune-
New York News Syndicate.

36. Rudolph Dirks,
"The Captain and
the Kids," 1940.
© United Feature Syndicate.

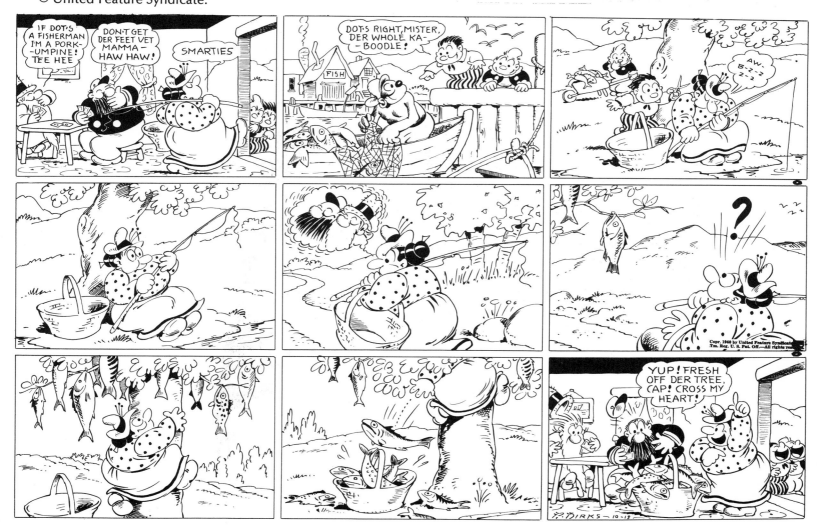

37. Crockett Johnson, "Barnaby," 1942. © Crockett Johnson.

38. Al Capp,

"Li'l Abner," 1949.

© United Feature Syndicate.

Man and Superman

Illustrations 39—64

The advent of the adventure-strip was the most significant development of the thirties and forties. The adventure series constituted a radical departure from the early features not only in theme but in style. They introduced into the comics a whole gallery of hero-images; and their success spawned a new medium: the comic-book, whose position was assured with the mighty assist of Superman and the cohorts of super-heroes he inspired.

WASH TUBBS   Out for Revenge   5-21   By Crane

WASH TUBBS   To the Finish   5-24   By Crane

WASH TUBBS   Beginning to Get Mad   5-25   By Crane

WASH TUBBS   Serves Him Right   5-26   By Crane

39. Roy Crane, "Wash Tubbs," 1928. © NEA Service.

40. Phillip Nowlan and Richard Calkins, "Buck Rogers," 1929. © National Newspaper Syndicate.

Tarzan

THE PHARAOH'S DAUGHTER.

by EDGAR RICE BURROUGHS

WHEN ALL HAD DEPARTED, ERICH VON HARBEN STILL LAY UNCONSCIOUS ON THE STAIRCASE LEADING TO THE APES' PIT.

AND NIKOTRIS, THE DAUGHTER OF THE PHARAOH, SAW HIM.

TENDERLY SHE KNELT BESIDE HIM AND FOUND THAT HE STILL LIVED.

AT HER COMMAND A LITTER WAS BROUGHT AND VON HARBEN WAS CARRIED TO THE GREAT OUTDOOR HOSPITAL.

THAT NIGHT NIKOTRIS PRAYED TO PENETER-DEVA (THE PLANET VENUS) TO MAKE THE STRANGER WELL.

RAPIDLY HE RECOVERED AND RAPIDLY HE LEARNED TO TALK IN EGYPTIAN TO THE FAIR NIKOTRIS, WHO CAME DAILY TO SEE HIM.

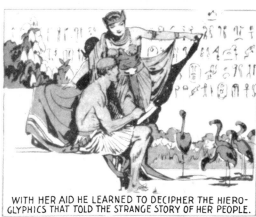

WITH HER AID HE LEARNED TO DECIPHER THE HIEROGLYPHICS THAT TOLD THE STRANGE STORY OF HER PEOPLE.

MEANWHILE, TARZAN, WHO HAD BEEN BROUGHT INTO THE SECRET CONFINES OF THE TEMPLE, SAW THE HIGH PRIEST POUR THE BURNING PITCH INTO AN OPENING IN THE PAVEMENT.

BELOW IN A DUNGEON PRISONERS WERE CHAINED.

WHEN THE BURNING PITCH FLAMED DOWN UPON ONE OF THEM....

....THE PRISONER HEARD THE HIGH PRIEST CRY, "SO THE GODS PUNISH TRAITORS!" BUT TARZAN UNDERSTOOD NOT AND HE FOLLOWED THE HIGH PRIEST UNTIL........

.....THE HIGH PRIEST SUDDENLY KNELT, OPENED A DOOR IN THE FLOOR, AND POINTED....TARZAN DREW BACK, STARTLED AT WHAT HE SAW.

NEXT WEEK:
TO THE GOD OF THE APES

41. Harold Foster, "Tarzan," 1933. © United Feature Syndicate.

1 SYNOPSIS
THE PAUPER PRINCE CAPTURES AND TRAINS A WILD HORSE, CONSTRUCTS HIS OWN HARNESS AND LEATHERN ARMOR, THEN SETS OUT TO BECOME A KNIGHT. AFTER WANDERING INLAND FOR SOME DAYS HE IS OVERTAKEN BY SIR GAWAIN, A KNIGHT OF THE ROUND TABLE.

2 IMPRESSED ALIKE BY VAL'S FEARLESS BEARING AND THE SMELL OF HIS COOKING, SIR GAWAIN ALIGHTS.

3 FROM HIS CONVERSATION VAL LEARNS MUCH OF THE LIFE AND DUTIES OF A KNIGHT.

4 AN ARMED KNIGHT AND HIS SQUIRE COME UP BEHIND THEM-- QUIETLY.

5 "'TIS SIR NEGARTH, A ROBBER KNIGHT," SAID SIR GAWAIN RECOGNIZING HIM AND REACHING FOR HIS SWORD.

6 BUT BEFORE HE COULD DRAW THE FALSE KNIGHT STRIKES HIM DOWN WITH HIS MACE!

7 "STRIP HIM AND LOAD HIS GEAR ON HIS HORSE."

8 NOT THE PROPER WAY TO VANQUISH A KNIGHT, BUT QUITE EFFECTIVE.

9 PRINCE VAL NEATLY SKEWERS THE CHARGING SQUIRE.

10 ""S 'DEATH," MARVELS THE KNIGHT, "I FIND A GOOD COOK, A PROTECTOR AND A BLOOD-THIRSTY HUMORIST ALL IN A DAY."

NEXT WEEK: "THE DRAGON"

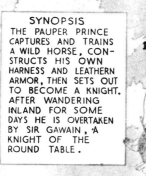

42. Harold Foster, "Prince Valiant," 1937. © King Features Syndicate.

Flash Gordon

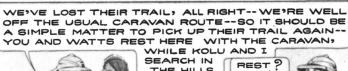

44. Alex Raymond, "Jungle Jim," 1937. © King Features Syndicate.

Flash Gordon

45. Alex Raymond,

"Flash Gordon," 1937.

© King Features Syndicate

— NEXT WEEK —
A DARING PLAN

Flash Gordon

46. Alex Raymond,

"Flash Gordon," 1938.

© King Features Syndicate

NEXT WEEK — **TROUBLE AHEAD**

47. Noel Sickles,
"Scorchy Smith," 1935.
© AP Feature Service.

48. William Ritt and Clarence Gray,
"Brick Bradford," 1935.
© King Features Syndicate.

49. Milton Caniff, "Terry and the Pirates," 1935. © Chicago Tribune-New York News Syndicate.

50. Milton Caniff, "Terry and the Pirates," 1944. © Chicago Tribune-New York News Syndicate.

51. Lee Falk and Phil Davis,
"Mandrake," 1936.
© King Features Syndicate.

52. Lee Falk and Ray Moore,
"The Phantom," 1938.
© King Features Syndicate.

53. Burne Hogarth, ''Drago,'' 1946. © N.Y. Post Corporation.

54. Chester Gould, "Dick Tracy," 1948. © Chicago Tribune-New York News Syndicate.

55. Jerry Siegel and Joe Shuster, "Superman," 1939. © National Periodical Publications.

56. Wayne Boring, "Superman," 1954. © National Periodical Publications.

Tarzan

by EDGAR RICE BURROUGHS

WITH RIMALI AND HIS PARTY ON THE TRAIL AGAIN TOWARD THALIA, TARZAN TOOK TO THE TREES, RANGING FAR AHEAD OF HIS COMPANIONS. SUDDENLY HE PAUSED----

--AND PEERED DOWN AT THE TRAIL BELOW. A GREAT BEAST MOVED SILENTLY ALONG THE TRAIL..... A LION---BEAUTIFULLY MANED AND BRILLIANTLY SPOTTED.

KEEPING PACE WITH THE LION, TARZAN SOON DISCOVERED THE PREY NUMA WAS STALKING.

CONTRARY TO THE HABIT OF MOST CARNIVORE ABOUT TO MAKE A KILL, THE SPOTTED LION SPRANG TOWARD ITS PREY IN UTTER SILENCE.

ALERTLY WATCHING THE DRAMA, TARZAN LEAPED IN THE PATH OF THE CHARGING FURY.

AS NUMA RENEWED THE ATTACK, TARZAN WHEELED, AND LEAPED FOR THE GREAT BEAST'S BACK.
2-6
HOGARTH

57. Burne Hogarth, "Tarzan," 1949. © United Feature Syndicate.

Scorchy Smith

No Sooner Said Than Seen

Scorchy Smith

One-Legged Landing

Scorchy Smith

Whatever Goes Up—!

58. Frank Robbins, "Scorchy Smith," 1939. © AP Feature Service.

59. Carl Burgos,

"The Human Torch," 1940.

© Marvel Comics Group.

60. Joe Simon and Jack Kirby,

"Captain America," 1941.

© Marvel Comics Group.

61. Will Eisner,
    "The Spirit," 1949.
    © Will Eisner.

62. Will Eisner,
    "The Spirit," 1949.
    © Will Eisner.

63. Bob Kane,
    "Batman," 1954.
    © National Periodical Publications.

64. William Marston,
    "Wonder Woman," 1954.
    © National Periodical Publications.

The Current Scene

Illustrations 65–78

In spite of the contributions made by the sophisticated and often wryly intellectual comic strips of the fifties ("Pogo" and "Peanuts" foremost among them), there has been a slow and steady artistic erosion, soon followed by an economic decline, first in the newspaper strip, and in the comic-book shortly afterwards. The paucity of worthwhile new features to come out of the sixties testifies to the desiccation of these forms.

65. Walt Kelly, "Pogo," 1959. © Walt Kelly.

66. Roy Crane, "Buz Sawyer," 1950. © King Features Syndicate.

67. Jules Feiffer, "Feiffer," 1960. © Jules Feiffer.

68. Leonard Starr, "On Stage," 1964. © Chicago Tribune-New York News Syndicate.

69. Mell Lazarus, "Miss Peach," 1959. © Publishers-Hall Syndicate.

70. Milton Caniff, "Steve Canyon," 1964. © Publishers-Hall Syndicate.

71. Johnny Hart, "B.C.," 1959. © Publishers-Hall Syndicate.

MARY WORTH

ALGER... IS STILL **ALIVE**?

HE WOULD HAVE COME HERE TO TELL YOU, HIMSELF, MRS. HARDIN, BUT IT SEEMED MORE CONSIDERATE TO HAVE SOMEONE ELSE TALK WITH YOU FIRST!

WHILE ALGER CLARK WAITS DOWNSTAIRS, MARY HAS BROKEN THE NEWS TO HIS FORMER MOTHER-IN-LAW AND HER SPINSTER SISTER.

WHO IS ALGER, AUNT HATTIE?

NEVER MIND, DEAR!... WE'LL EXPLAIN IT ALL TO YOU... SOMETIME!

YOUR DAUGHTER'S HUSBAND FELL THAT DAY WHILE HUNTING, MRS. HARDIN!.... WHEN HE...REGAINED HIS FACULTIES...HE WAS HUNDREDS OF MILES FROM HOME!

AND WHY DIDN'T HE COMMUNICATE **AT ONCE** WITH IVA, MRS. WORTH?

HE HAD SUFFERED A COMPLETE LAPSE OF MEMORY!

AMNESIA?... **BAH!**... THE FAVORITE PLOT DEVICE OF THE **LAZY FICTION WRITER**, MRS. WORTH!

...AND THE FIRST EXCUSE A **RUNAWAY HUSBAND** THINKS OF...WHEN HE HAS GROWN TIRED OF MEETING HIS FAMILY RESPONSIBILITIES!

YES!... I REMEMBER ONCE VISITING HIM AND IVA...WHEN THEY WERE EXPECTING LITTLE BERTIE...AND HE WAS WORRIED FOR FEAR THEY COULDN'T **AFFORD** A CHILD!

Publishers Newspaper Syndicate, 1966

I HAVE EVERY REASON TO BELIEVE THAT MR. CLARK IS TELLING THE **TRUTH**, MISS FROST!

HMPF!... SENDING **A COMPLETE STRANGER** HERE WITH HIS STORY HARDLY INDICATES THAT!

I'VE HAD CONSIDERABLE EXPERIENCE IN JUDGING HUMAN BEHAVIOR, MISS FROST...AND MR. CLARK WAS NOT **ACTING** WHEN HE REALIZED HIS SECOND MARRIAGE MIGHT BE...

MRS. WORTH!...ARE YOU SAYING THAT ALGER **MARRIED** AGAIN?!

6-5-66

72. Ken Ernst and Allen Saunders, "Mary Worth," 1966. © Publishers-Hall Syndicate.

73. Charles Schulz,
"Peanuts," 1967.
© United Feature Syndicate.

beetle bailey — by mort Walker

74. Mort Walker, "Beetle Bailey," 1968. © King Features Syndicate.

75. Wallace Wood, "Animan," 1968. © Wallace Wood.

82

76. Stan Lee and Jack Kirby,
    ''The Mighty Thor,'' 1966.
    © Marvel Comics Group.

77. Al Williamson,
    ''Flash Gordon,'' 1967.
    © King Features Syndicate.

78. Roy Thomas and Neal Adams, "X-Men," 1969. © Marvel Comics Group.

The Faraway
and the Far-Out

Illustrations 79–98

Art, like nature, abhors a vacuum. After fifty years of almost unrelieved mediocrity, the European comics have reached during the last two decades a level of artistic excellence rarely found nowadays in the American comics. Closer to home, the "underground" comics (or comix) have renewed the great iconoclastic tradition of the early "funnies" that the "establishment" cartoonists seem to have abandoned in favor of middle-class dullness.

... profit cette solitude momentanée pour opérer un changement de décor à vue. Retirant avec ensemble leurs casquettes plates et leurs pèlerines boches, ils se coiffèrent du képi à feuillage de chêne en or des généraux français et Croquignol, afin de se vieillir, s'affubla d'une paire de moustaches blanches postiches qui contribuaient...

... à lui donner un air beaucoup plus martial. Lorsque cette transformation fut opérée, loin des regards indiscrets, l'auto poursuivant sa course longea le bois pendant quelques minutes et pénétra ensuite dans une clairière dans laquelle se trouvait une seconde auto arrêtée près d'une tente confortablement aménagée. « Sapristi ! nous ne sommes pas en avance ! constatait Filochard. Je vois que nous sommes attendus et que l'héritier du Kaiser est pressé de conclure cette paix telle que je la...

« ... lui laissais entrevoir hier lorsqu'il m'a reçu en audience... Attention ! Nous allons procéder au lancement du bateau. » Averti par le bruit du moteur, un homme venait de sortir de la tente et sa physionomie reflétait le superlatif de la satisfaction. C'était le Kronprinz. Suivant ce qui avait été convenu la veille entre Filochard et lui, il attendait...

... l'arrivée des deux généraux français à qui des pouvoirs avaient été délégués pour signer la paix. L'auto venait de s'arrêter à quelques pas du prince héritier. Filochard, quittant son siège, ouvrit la portière de l'auto à ses deux copains qui en descendirent avec une gravité de circonstance. Il présenta les deux généraux au Kronprinz qui leur souhaita gracieusement le bienvenue et ceux-ci répondirent à la cordialité de son accueil par un salut d'une correction parfaite. Sur l'invitation du fils à Guillaume, ils pénétrèrent sous la tente. Aussitôt...

... la discussion commença. Les généraux avouèrent sans difficulté que la France souffrait de la guerre et qu'ils avaient reçu mission de traiter les conditions de paix. « Nous n'irons pas par quatre chemins, déclarait Croquignol. Nous vous donnons la Belgique, la Hollande, la Grèce, le Congo, l'Egypte et la Pologne ainsi qu'une indemnité de cent milliards, à la condition que vous suspendrez immédiatement les hostilités. Vous voyez que nous sommes ronds en affaires et nous...

« ... espérons que vous nous en tiendrez compte. » Le Kronprinz, abasourdi, n'en pouvait croire ses oreilles et tirait sur les soies de ses moustaches pour s'assurer qu'il ne rêvait pas. C'était à l'heure où l'Allemagne affamée et moralement vaincue se disposait à capituler que la France lui offrait cette paix si glorieusement avantageuse. « Och ! jubilait-il, quelle veine pour moi de traiter dans de telles conditions ! Papa va en baver ! » Le traité de paix fut donc signé d'emblée et le Kronprinz affirma : « Messieurs, à partir de...

« ... demain, les hostilités seront suspendues. Je vous suis reconnaissant de la façon dont cette paix a été signée. Avec la France, si chevaleresque et si généreuse, il y a toujours moyen de s'entendre. » Croquignol, Ribouldingue et Filochard avaient bien du mal à garder leur sérieux. N'y pouvant tenir davantage, ils remontèrent précipitamment en auto et repartirent en quatrième vitesse, laissant le Kronprinz mariner dans la joie la plus kolossale. Ah ! le rejeton du Kaiser avait admirablement marché et coupé dans le panneau. Aveuglé par sa stupide vanité, il s'était naïvement imaginé avoir remporté un triomphal succès et croyait que c'était arrivé.

C'est dire qu'il était à cent lieues de se douter du piège dans lequel les Pieds-Nickelés avaient réussi à le faire tomber. Il ne devait point tarder à s'en apercevoir à ses dépens et le sourire de bonheur qu'il esquissait allait bientôt se changer en affreuse grimace !

79. Louis Forton, (France), "Les Pieds Nickelés," 1916. © Editions Azur.

80. André Franquin, *(Belgium)*, "Spirou," 1960. © Editions Dupuis.

81. Hergé (Georges Rémi), (Belgium), "Tintin," 1939. © Editions Casterman.

82. Alain Saint-Ogan, *(France)*, "Zig et Puce," 1948. © Alain Saint-Ogan.

83. Edgar-Pierre Jacobs, (Belgium), "Le Piège Diabolique," 1962. © Editions du Lombard.

84. Greg *(Michel Regnier)*, *(France)*, "Achille Talon," 1963. © Editions Dargaud.

85. Jean-Claude Forest, *(France)*, "Barbarella," 1963. © Le Terrain Vague.

86. René Goscinny and Albert Uderzo, *(France)*, "Asterix," 1965. © Editions Dargaud.

87. James Holdaway, *(England)*, ''Modesty Blaise,'' 1967. © London Evening Standard.

88. Peyo *(Pierre Culliford),*
    (Belgium), "Les Schtroumpfs," 1967.
    © Editions Dupuis.

89. Jijé *(Joseph Gillain), (France),*
    "le Spécialiste," 1970. © Johnny.

90. Ugo Pratt, *(Italy)*, ''Una Ballata del Mare Salato,'' 1968. © Sgt. Kirk.

91. Hermann *(Hermann Huppen)* and Greg, *(Belgium)*, "Bernard Prince," 1969. © Editions du Lombard.

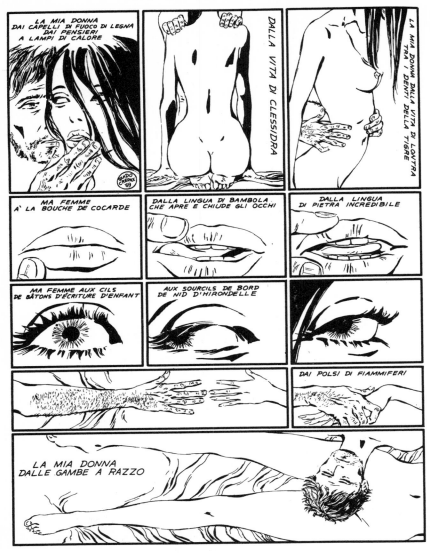

92. Guido Crepax, *(Italy)*,
"La Casa Matta," 1969. © E.D.I.P.

93. Gilbert Shelton, "The Fabulous
Furry Freak Brothers," 1968. © Gilbert Shelton.

94. Robert Crumb, "Mr. Natural," 1967. © Robert Crumb.

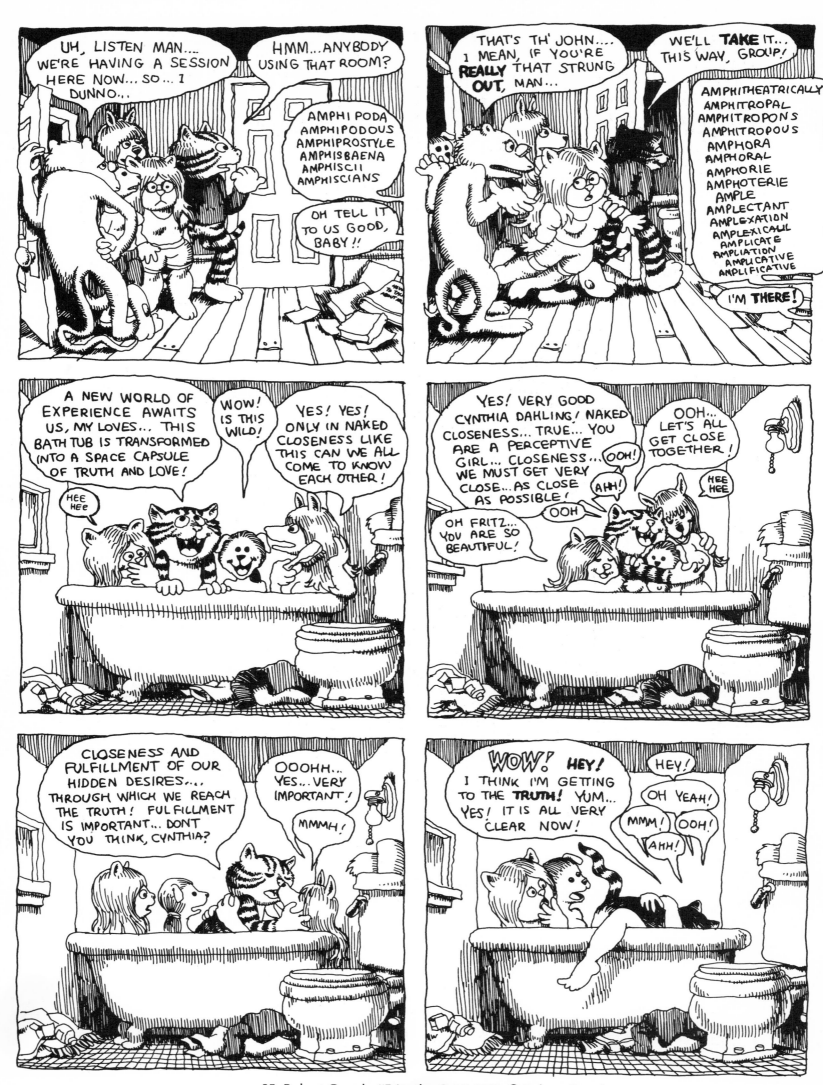

95. Robert Crumb, "Fritz the Cat," 1968. © Robert Crumb.

96. Art Spiegelman, "Quentin Fester," 1969. © Art Spiegelman.

97. Jay Lynch,
   "Nard n' Pat," 1970.
   © Bijou Publishing Empire.

98. Skip Williamson,
   "Ragtime Billy," 1970.
   © Bijou Publishing Empire.

Illustrations

The illustrations in this volume are included in the New York Cultural Center exhibition, *75 Years of the Comics,* and were selected by Maurice Horn, consultant for the exhibition. All illustrations are from Mr. Horn's collection unless otherwise stated.

COVER: Richard Felton Outcault, *The Great Dog Show in M'Googan Avenue* (1896). This is the historic *Yellow Kid* (February 16, 1896), credited with having initiated a new art form, called later "the comics." Courtesy of Richard Marshall.

BACK COVER: Winsor McCay, *Little Nemo in Slumberland* (1906).

FRONTISPIECE: Richard Felton Outcault, *Buster Brown* (1908). This original drawing was presented to Colonel William Cody ("Buffalo Bill") in 1908. Courtesy of the Buffalo Bill Memorial Museum, Golden, Colorado.

The Heroic Period

1. Image d'Epinal, *(France),* 19th Century.
2. Rodolphe Töpffer, *(Switzerland),* "Monsieur Crépin," 1846.
3. Wilhelm Busch, *(Germany),* "Max und Moritz," 1871.
4. Christophe, *(Georges Colomb), (France),* "La Famille Fenouillard," 1893.
5. Richard F. Outcault, "The Yellow Kid," 1896.
6. James Swinnerton, "Little Tiger," 1901.
7. Rudolph Dirks, "The Katzenjammer Kids," 1901.
8. Frederick Burr Opper, "Happy Hooligan," 1901.
9. Gustave Verbeck. "The Upside-Downs of Little Lady Lovekins and Old Man Muffaroo," 1903.
10. James Swinnerton, "'Little Jimmy," 1905.
11. Silas *(Winsor McCay),* "The Dream of the Rarebit Fiend," 1905.
12. Winsor McCay, "Little Nemo," 1906.
13. Winsor McCay, "Little Nemo," 1907.
14. Lyonel Feininger, "Wee Willie Winkie's World," 1906.
15. Lyonel Feininger, "The Kin-der Kids," 1906.
16. Richard F. Outcault, "Buster Brown," 1907.

The Great Tradition

17. George McManus, "Bringing Up Father," 1921. © King Features Syndicate.
18. George McManus, "Bringing Up Father," 1932. © King Features Syndicate.
19. Rube Goldberg, "Boob McNutt," 1920. © King Features Syndicate.
20. Harold H. Knerr, "The Katzenjammer Kids," 1924. © King Features Syndicate.
21. Willy DeBeck, "Barney Google," 1924. © King Features Syndicate.

22. Milton Gross, "Nize Baby," 1926. © New York World.

23. Harold Gray, "Little Orphan Annie," 1926. © Chicago Tribune-New York News Syndicate.

24. Sidney Smith, "The Gumps," 1927 © Chicago Tribune-New York News Syndicate.

25. Martin Branner, "Winnie Winkle," 1927. © Chicago Tribune-New York News Syndicate.

26. Frank King, "Gasoline Alley," 1928. © Chicago Tribune-New York News Syndicate.

27. H. C. "Bud" Fisher, "Mutt and Jeff," 1930. © H. C. Fisher.

28. Frank Godwin, "Connie," 1931. © Frank Godwin.

29. Chic Young, "Blondie," 1933. © King Features Syndicate.

30. Chic Young, "Blondie," 1948. © King Features Syndicate.

31. Lyman Young, "The Kid Sister," 1933. © King Features Syndicate.

32. George Herriman, "Krazy Kat," 1937. © King Features Syndicate.

33. George Herriman, "Krazy Kat," 1941. © King Features Syndicate.

34. Elzie Segar, "Popeye," 1935. © King Features Syndicate.

35. Frank Willard, "Moon Mullins," 1937. © Chicago Tribune-New York News Syndicate.

36. Rudolph Dirks, "The Captain and the Kids," 1940. © United Feature Syndicate.

37. Crockett Johnson, "Barnaby," 1942. © Crockett Johnson.

38. Al Capp, "Li'l Abner," 1949. © United Feature Syndicate.

Man and Superman

39. Roy Crane, "Wash Tubbs," 1928. © NEA Service, courtesy of Bill Blackbeard.

40. Phillip Nowlan and Richard Calkins, "Buck Rogers," 1929. © National Newspaper Syndicate.

41. Harold Foster, "Tarzan," 1933. © United Feature Syndicate.

42. Harold Foster, "Prince Valiant," 1937. © King Features Syndicate, courtesy of Tony Sanguino.

43. Alex Raymond, "Flash Gordon," 1934. © King Features Syndicate.

44. Alex Raymond, "Jungle Jim," 1937. © King Features Syndicate.

45. Alex Raymond, "Flash Gordon," 1937. © King Features Syndicate.

46. Alex Raymond, "Flash Gordon," 1938. © King Features Syndicate.

47. Noel Sickles, "Scorchy Smith," 1935. © AP Feature Service.

48. William Ritt and Clarence Gray, "Brick Bradford," 1935. © King Features Syndicate.

49. Milton Caniff, "Terry and the Pirates," 1935. © Chicago Tribune-New York News Syndicate.

50. Milton Caniff, "Terry and the Pirates," 1944. © Chicago Tribune-New York News Syndicate.

51. Lee Falk and Phil Davis, "Mandrake," 1936. © King Features Syndicate.

52. Lee Falk and Ray Moore, "The Phantom," 1938. © King Features Syndicate.

53. Burne Hogarth, "Drago," 1946. © N.Y. Post Corporation.

54. Chester Gould, "Dick Tracy," 1948. © Chicago Tribune-New York News Syndicate.

55. Jerry Siegel and Joe Shuster, "Superman," 1939. © National Periodical Publications.

56. Wayne Boring, "Superman," 1954. © National Periodical Publications.

57. Burne Hogarth, "Tarzan," 1949. © United Feature Syndicate.

58. Frank Robbins, "Scorchy Smith," 1939. © AP Feature Service.

59. Carl Burgos, "The Human Torch," 1940. © Marvel Comics Group.

60. Joe Simon and Jack Kirby, "Captain America," 1941. © Marvel Comics Group.

61. Will Eisner, "The Spirit," 1949. © Will Eisner.

62. Will Eisner, "The Spirit," 1949. © Will Eisner.

63. Bob Kane, "Batman," 1954. © National Periodical Publication.

64. William Marston, "Wonder Woman," 1954. © National Periodical Publications.

The Current Scene

65. Walt Kelly, "Pogo," 1959. © Walt Kelly.

66. Roy Crane, "Buz Sawyer," 1950. © King Features Syndicate.

67. Jules Feiffer, "Feiffer," 1960. © Jules Feiffer.

68. Leonard Starr, "On Stage," 1964. © Chicago Tribune-New York News Syndicate.

69. Mell Lazarus, "Miss Peach," 1959. © Publishers-Hall Syndicate.

70. Milton Caniff, "Steve Canyon," 1964. © Publishers-Hall Syndicate.

71. Johnny Hart, "B.C.," 1959. © Publishers-Hall Syndicate.

72. Ken Ernst and Allen Saunders, "Mary Worth," 1966. © Publishers-Hall Syndicate.

73. Charles Schulz, "Peanuts," 1967. © United Feature Syndicate.

74. Mort Walker, "Beetle Bailey," 1968. © King Features Syndicate.

75. Wallace Wood, "Animan," 1968. © Wallace Wood.

76. Stan Lee and Jack Kirby, "The Mighty Thor," 1966. © Marvel Comics Group.

77. Al Williamson, "Flash Gordon," 1967. © King Features Syndicate.

78. Roy Thomas and Neal Adams, "X-Men," 1969. © Marvel Comics Group.

The Faraway and the Far-out

79. Louis Forton, (France), "Les Pieds Nickelés," 1916. © Editions Azur.

80. André Franquin, (Belgium), "Spirou," 1960. © Editions Dupuis.

81. Hergé (Georges Rémi), (Belgium), "Tintin," 1939. © Editions Casterman.

82. Alain Saint-Ogan, (France), "Zig et Puce," 1948. © Alain Saint-Ogan.

83. Edgar-Pierre Jacobs, (Belgium), "Le Piège Diabolique," 1962. © Editions du Lombard.

84. Greg (Michel Regnier), (France), "Achille Talon," 1963. © Editions Dargaud.

85. Jean-Claude Forest, (France), "Barbarella," 1963. © Le Terrain Vague.

86. René Goscinny and Albert Uderzo, (France), "Asterix," 1965. © Editions Dargaud.

87. James Holdaway, (England), "Modesty Blaise," 1967. © London Evening Standard.

88. Peyo (Pierre Culliford), (Belgium), "Les Schtroumpfs," 1967. © Editions Dupuis.

89. Jijé (Joseph Gillain), (France), "le Spécialiste," 1970. © Johnny.

90. Ugo Pratt, (Italy), "Una Ballata del Mare Salato," 1968. © Sgt. Kirk.

91. Hermann (Hermann Huppen) and Greg, (Belgium), "Bernard Prince," 1969. © Editions du Lombard.

92. Guido Crepax, (Italy), "La Casa Matta," 1969. © E.D.I.P.

93. Gilbert Shelton, "The Fabulous Furry Freak Brothers," 1968. © Gilbert Shelton.

94. Robert Crumb, "Mr. Natural," 1967. © Robert Crumb.

95. Robert Crumb, "Fritz the Cat," 1968. © Robert Crumb.

96. Art Spiegelman, "Quentin Fester," 1969. © Art Spiegelman.

97. Jay Lynch, "Nard n' Pat," 1970. © Bijou Publishing Empire.

98. Skip Williamson, "Ragtime Billy," 1970. © Bijou Publishing Empire.

Selected Bibliography

Only books and articles dealing with some general aspect of the comics are listed. Monographs on particular authors, features, press releases, promotional pieces, or other topical material are omitted.

BOOKS IN ENGLISH

Abel, Robert H., and David Manning White, editors, *The Funnies: An American Idiom*. New York: The Free Press of Glencoe, 1963.

Aldridge, Alan, and George Perry, *The Penguin Book of Comics*. Harmsworth, England: Penguin Books, 1967.

Becker, Stephen, *Comic Art in America*. New York: Simon and Schuster, 1959.

Couperie, Pierre, and Maurice Horn, *A History of the Comic Strip*. New York: Crown, 1968.

Craven, Thomas, *Cartoon Cavalcade*. New York: Simon and Schuster, 1943.

Davidson, Sol, *Culture and the Comic Strip*. New York: New York University, 1959. Ph.D. thesis.

Feiffer, Jules, *The Great Comic Book Heroes*. New York; Dial Press, 1965.

Lupoff, Richard, and Donald Thompson, editors, *All in Color for a Dime*. New Rochelle, N.Y.: Arlington House, 1970.

Murrel, William A., *A History of American Graphic Humor*. New York: Macmillan, for the Whitney Museum of American Art (two volumes), 1933 and 1938.

Sheridan, Martin, *Comics and Their Creators: Life Stories of American Cartoonists*. Boston: Hale, Cushman and Flint, 1942.

Waugh, Coulton, *The Comics*. New York: Macmillan, 1947.

Wertham, Frederic, *Seduction of the Innocent*, New York: Rinehart & Co., 1954.

BOOKS IN OTHER LANGUAGES

Blanchard, Gérard, *La Bande Dessinée*, Verviers: Editions Marabout, 1969.

Caen, Michel, with Jacques Lob and Jacques Sternberg, *Les Chefs d'Oeuvre de la Bande Dessinée*. Paris: Planète, 1967.

Caradec, François, *I Primi Eroi*. Milan: Garzanti, 1962.

Della Corte, Carlo, *I Fumetti*. Milan: Mondadori, 1961.

Gasca, Luis, *Los Comics en la Pantalla*. San Sebastian: Festival Internacional del Cine, 1965.

Lipscyc, Enrique, *La Historieta Mundial*. Buenos Aires: Editorial Lipscyc, 1958.

Peignot, Joseph, *Les Copains de Votre Enfance*. Paris: Denoël, 1963.

ARTICLES AND PAMPHLETS

André, Jean-Claude, "Esthétique des Bandes Dessinées," *Revue d'Esthétique*, tome XVIII, fascicule I, 1965.

Arbuthnot, M. H., "Children and the Comics," *Elementary English Review*, March, 1947.

Augusto, Sergio, "As Bandas Francesas," *Jornal do Brasil,* March 3, 1967.

——————, "Quadrinho é Coisa Cada Vez Mais Séria," *Visao,* March 4, 1966.

Barcus, Francis Earle, "A Content Analysis of Trends in Sunday Comics, 1900-1955," *Journalism Quarterly,* Spring 1961, University of Minnesota.

Benayoun, Robert, *"Le Ballon dans les Bandes Dessinées."* Paris: André Balland, 1968.

Bertieri, Claudio, "Banda Stagnata e Banda Disegnata," *Finsider,* no. 6, October, 1967.

——————, "Comics e Video," *Linus,* no. 25, April, 1966.

Brackman, Jacob, "The Great International Comix Conspiracy," *Playboy,* December, 1970.

Broun, Heywood, "Wham! and Pow! the Comic Strip," *New Republic,* May 17, 1939.

Caen Michel, "Comic-strip et Celluloïde," *Les Lettres Françaises,* no. 1138, June 30-July 6, 1966.

Calisi, Romano, "Stampa a Fumetti, Cultura di Massa, Società Contemporanea," *Quaderni di Comunicazioni di Massa,* no. 1, 1965.

Caniff, Milton, "Don't Laugh at the Comics," *Cosmopolitan,* November, 1958.

Capp, Al, "The Case for the Comics," *Saturday Review of Literature,* March, 1948.

Couperie, Pierre, Des Suppléments du Dimanche aux Journaux Illustrés," *Giff-Wiff,* no. 8, 1963.

——————, "100.000.000 de Lieues en Ballon," catalogue of exhibition "Science-Fiction," Kunsthalle, Bern, 1967.

Della Corte, Carlo, "I Comics in Italia, Oggi," *Almanacco Letterario Bompiani,* 1963.

Eco, Umberto, "Il Mito di Superman e la Dissoluzione del Tempo," *Archivio di Filosofia,* 1-2, 1962.

——————, "La Stuttura Iterativa dei Fumetti," *Quaderni di Comunicazioni di Massa,* no. 1, 1965.

Fermigier, André, "Bande Dessinée et Sociologie," *Le Nouvel Observateur,* April 19, 1967.

Fouilhé, Pierre, "La Presse Enfantine," *L'Ecole des Parents,* no. 10, March, 1965.

Gaines, M. C., "Narrative Illustration of Comics," *Print Magazine,* vol. III, no. 2, August, 1942.

Gasca, Luis, "Elogio del Tebeo," *Véteres,* December 1, 1962.

——————, "Historia y Anécdota del Tebeo en España," *Diputación de Zaragoza,* 1965.

Greg, Michel, "La Bande Dessinée, Phénomène Social?" catalogue of exhibition "Introduction à la Bande Dessinée Belge," Bibliothèque Royale de Belgique, 1968.

Hegerfors, Sture, "Svisch! Pow! Sock! Seriernas Fantastika Värld," *Bokförlage Corona,* Lund, Sweden, 1966.

Horn, Maurice, "The Adventure Strip," introduction to *Flash Gordon,* New York: Nostalgia Press, 1967.

——————, "Comics USA," *Tintin,* nos. 30-34, July 28-August 25, 1970.

——————, "Histoire de la Bande Dessinée," *Informations et Documents,* no. 243, May, 1967.

——————, "70 Années de Bandes Dessinées," *Phénix,* no. 1, October, 1966.

Kelly, Walt, "Pogo Looks at the Abominable Snowman," *Saturday Review,* August 30, 1958.

Lacassin, Francis, "La Bande Dessinée," *Oeuvres Laïques de la Seine,* nos. 92-93, November-December, 1967.

————————, "Rien n'est vrai, Tout est permis," *Les Lettres Françaises*, no. 1138, June 30-July 6, 1966.

Latona, Robert, "Comics: Castro Style," *Vanguard*, no. 1, 1966.

Martin, Antonio, "Apuntes para una Historia de los Tebeos. I. Los periódicos para la Infancia (1833-1917)," *Revista de Educación*, no. 194, December, 1967.

————————, "Apuntes para una Historia de los Tebeos. II. La Civilización de la Imagen," *Revista de Educación*, no. 195, January, 1968.

Mattingly, Ignatius G., "Some Cultural Aspects of Serial Cartoons, or Get a Load of Those Funnies," *Harper's*, December, 1955.

Millo, Stelio, "Appunti sul Fumetto Fascista," *Linus*, no. 10, 1966.

Pennel, Elizabeth R., "Our Tragic Comics," *North American Review*, February, 1920.

Politzer, Heinz, "From Little Nemo to Li'l Abner," *Commentary*, October, 1949.

Quennell, P., "Comic Strips in England: Future Folklorists Will Find in Them the Mythology of the Present Day," *Living Age*, March, 1941.

Sadoul, Georges, "Le Cinéma et les Bandes Dessinées," *Les Lettres Françaises*, no. 1138, June 30-July 6, 1966.

Seldes, Gilbert, "Some Sour Commentators: Comics Artists," *New Republic*, June 10, 1925.

Traini, Rinaldo, and Sergio Trinchero, "I Fumetti," *Enciclopedia del Tempo Libero*, May, 1968.

Van Gelder, Lindsay, and Lawrence, "The Radicalization of the Superheroes," *New York*, October 19, 1970.

Welke, Manfred, "Die Sprache der Comics," Frankfurt: Dipa Verlag, 1958.

Winterbotham, Russell Robert, "How Comic Strips Are Made," Girard, Kansas: Haldemann-Julius, 1946.

Zorbaugh, Harvey, "Comics—There They Stand," *Journal of Educational Sociology*, December, 1944.

DATE DUE